Hari Singh Nalwa

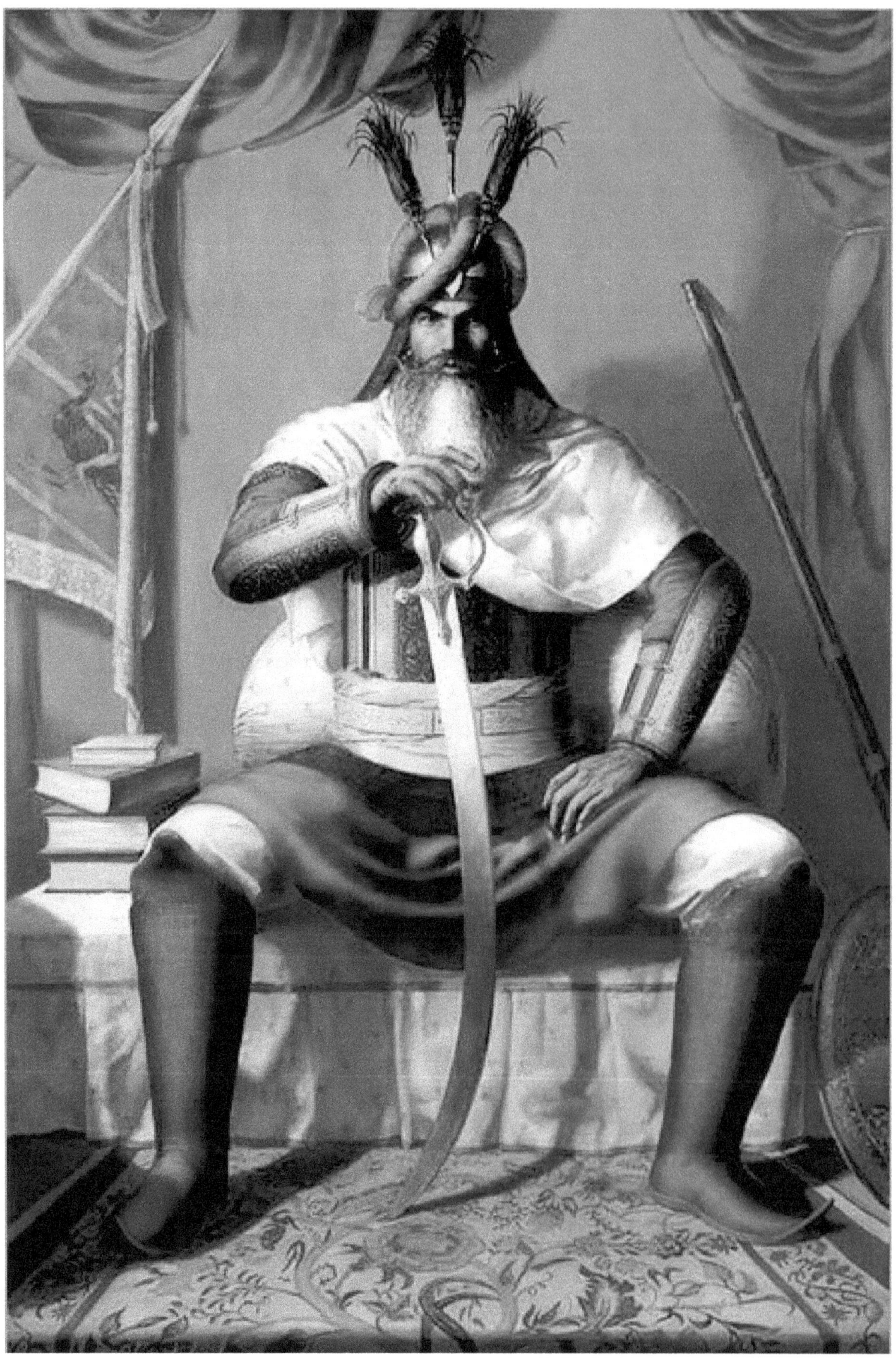

Punjab is the land of heroes. The pages of history bear witness to the fact that from ancient times whenever the Jarwanis of the west looked towards India with a keen eye and rushed here to climb it, Did and frowned.

Alexander the Great, the world-conquering emperor of Greece, had left Rome and Syria in turmoil, crushed Iraq and Iran, and crushed Afghanistan. But they were. Poor. When in India he clashed with some of the warriors of Majha and the eastern Punjab, even his great warriors were devastated. The Punjabis took iron with the enemy for the sake of the sacred land of their country.

As the Greeks seemed to move forward, the Punjabis would become more and more stubborn. They would be doubly angry and would burn at the throat of the Greeks. The Greeks were suddenly discouraged. On the banks of the river Beasa they went straight to the bank and their piles collapsed. The Punjabis' flaming deadly swords, their spears piercing their chests and spears, and the shouts that shook the hundreds of heavens frightened the Greeks so much that they lost their heart and ran away. . Alexander's hopes of conquering the whole world were dashed and his dreams vanished in an instant. He killed many of his warriors.

He gave courage but he did not dare to stand in front of the dagger of Punjabis Half of the Punjab lay ahead. The last experience was so costly and bitter for the Greeks that they could not be prepared for another experiment. Armed with spears, spears and spears, the Punjabi Greeks began to look like angels of death, and again and again they remembered their home, mother, father, sisters, wives and children, and they reunited Alexander with the Greeks. But forced to return. But even then the Punjabis did not let him go. Near the confluence of Ravi and Jhans then Maloi Lank lived. They raided the restored Greek army and restored it. In an encounter with them about forty miles north-east of Multan, Alexander himself was wounded and knocked unconscious by an arrow in his chest. After crossing the Indus River, Alexander went straight to Greece, but on the way, Poo. He died at the site of Babylon in 607 BCE

Alexander could not establish a permanent state in the Punjab. As soon as he turned his face, there was an uproar and soon after his death, Chandra-Gupta (5-6 AD) left a large wallet of Greeks in the Punjab. BCE

When King Siks Niktaur of Syria invaded the Punjab, he had to give and take, and he left the area east of Sindh and his daughter Dola!

With the passage of time the skirts of the Kushan (Yu-chi) people on the west side became heavier for some time. The fact is that most people in the Indus Sea and Doaba have lions in front but not vultures. The louder the noise they make, the faster they push back when someone hits the front. That is why the Jarwanas across the west were quick to succeed in this area and it was easier for them to move forward. But in the beginning of the climb the backs may be soft, but when the anger rises and comes to its mother, the feet fall on the enemy like ferocious tigers and do not fall back until they kill the prey. The Kushan (Yu-chi) people remained in the area of Peshawar till 3 AD, when the whites had just beaten them to death, but in the Punjab it became difficult for them to stand firm and Hile Vasudev (2-2). After that his condition started getting thinner

The warriors quickly raised their heads and es -
tablished independent states on the left. Many
scholars agree that the credit for ending the Kushan
rule in the Punjab goes to the warriors. The area of the
warriors was south of the Sutlej as far as Haryana and
their capital was at Netak (Sunet near Ludhiana) and
on the coins issued by them was a statue of the god of
war Kartikeya. Due to the bravery of these warriors on
the battlefield, the meaning of the word warrior
became the beloved, fearless warrior and warrior of
the war.

.The heroism of the Punjabis and the courage to fight
with all their might to save the independence of the
country was feared. The brave Muslims could easily
establish their rule in India
Couldn't succeed quickly. The Islamic Mujahideen
(religious warriors) who in the eighty years after the
demise of Hazrat Muhammad Sahib. Europe's
footsteps reached Spain, attacked by Mohammed bin
Qasim
Three and a half hundred years from the time of Salkai
to the time of Sabkatgin Could not move towards
Punjab. After that Ghaznavis and Gauris got some The
success was due to the fact that they were

residents across the Indus and beyond
They had created fear by looting the people around.
He had also formed a community with a few people
and with their help he came forward. During the time
of Ghulam, Khalji, Tughlaq, Sayand and Lodhi
dynasties, many people became Muralmans and
became pro-Muslim. With this, the Mughals had a lot
to do in establishing their rule after the Landhis But
the unspeakable and unbearable atrocities of the
Mughal raids on the destitute and humiliated masses
of Punjab and the screams of the miserable miserable
people had such a profound effect on the mind of
Guru Nanak, the revolutionary saint of Punjab that he
became the voice of the masses.

It is not uncommon in the history of the world for a universal religious leader to have felt the plight of his countrymen and raised such a loud voice against the oppressive enemies and raised the hearts of the people.

On the Sumerian mountain when Guru Nanak was patrolling with the Siddhas and the Siddhas asked, 'Nanaka, what is happening in Mother Luck? Then AAP replied that there is darkness and sin in the world of India, the oppressed people are screaming, don't you listen to them. The so-called Siddhas are hiding in the mountains. The world is sinking without a true leader In this way Guru Nanak realized the plight of the country and awakened the people with his words and beautiful kirtan. The other Gur sahibs, following in their footsteps, tried to unite the people. Guru Hargobind instilled the spirit of war in the people of Punjab and Guru Gobind Singh, in direct confrontation with the Mughal Empire, raised the spirits of the people in such a way that the Khalsa under the leadership of Baba Banda Singh Bahadur liberated a large part of the rising Punjab under the yoke of the Mughals. After the martyrdom of Banda Singh, the Khalsa had to endure many years in the furnace of harshness and tyranny. Emperor Bahadur Shah issued orders for the massacre of Sikhs in December , killing Sikhs wherever they were found. This order was repeated in the time of Farkhsiyar. But is it any wonder that the Singhs have lost heart? With the order and strictness of every massacre, they grew bitterly and fought for new resistance.

When Nader Shah was on his way back to Iran, the Singhs came out of the Shivalak hills and started attacking him and took him to Iran. He saved a part of the wealth of India. Seeing this bravery of the Singhs, Nader Shah became furious. But he could not do anything. Singh would sometimes raid or kill in front, sometimes in the back and sometimes in between, and before the Iranians became aware, he would go to the trenches to fill the chugis and keep watching Nader Shah. Nader Shah, lying on the ground, asked Zakariya Khan, the governor of Lahore, "Who are these people who have come my way?" Has done and eaten my army too. I have conquered Iran, trampled Afghanistan and blown away the dust of Mughal rule. Please tell, whats the story of them . Zakariya Khan replied that they were followers of a unique religion. The forest is their country and the saddles of horses are their home. They sleep while standing and eat while walking and do not know the taste of cow dung. Neither water nor fire to warm the bones. We kill them by torturing them but they also accept him with pleasure. He is ready to fight with hundreds alone and he is not afraid of death. We are tired of beating them but these days are getting doubled day and night ... Hearing this Nader Shah smiled and said then be afraid of them. The time is not far when they will be beheaded and become the guardians of the country. The time of Zakariya Khan and his son Yahya Khan was one of the most tumultuous and oppressive in the history of Punjab, while thousands of Singhs were captured from villages and killed at Lahore Ghoramandi (Bazar Nakhas). In spite of all this, sometimes the lone Singh fought against the Mughals was standing as Banta Singh challenged the government of Lahore on the road near Tarn Taran and wrote a letter to Khan Bahadur Zakariya Khan that you understood the resolution that Singh has been killed, he is still alive Are standing firm against

As soon as Mir Mannu became the ruler of Lahore, he sent out patrol troops to the villages to kill the Singhs and captured and killed thousands. But Singh was coming out of the furnace of fire in the form of day and in the will of God, steadfast, fearless, contented in the will, was heard singing like this:

Give us our sickle, we give it to Mannu.

As the mind was cut off, we fell asleep. They believed that the time of oppression and misery did not last long, but the end of oppression and tyranny. If one does not waver and the pious one walks on his appointed path, no one can frighten him, no one can defeat him, no one can kill him. Happiness . According to the state of mind. Those who have faith in Akal in their mind, can never have any hot wind. They walk in the rising art all the time and with a smile on their face they face every a adversity and every enemy and the end that befalls them.

Be it the horse market of Lahore, or the hills of Jamrud and Saragarhi, Nifa or the fragmented area of Lakh, the Kashmir campaign or the confrontation with the Pakistanis They read and hear: It doesn't feel hot like Guru ka Singhs to the Kia Singhs-- I and when the war is over, the enemy seems to be falling, they pray to Akal Purakh and in these words of Guru Gobind Singh, :

" Dev Shiva bar mohe hai, shub karman te kabhu na taro, na daro ar so jab jae laro, nischa kar apni jit karo, ar sikh ha apne man ko hieh lalach hau gun tau uchro.'

Means don't be afraid, so when you go, make sure you win.

After the death of Mir Mannu, King Ahmad Shah Durrani of Afghanistan began his efforts to occupy the Punjab. But now the Singhs are leaping from the mountains to the north and out of the jungles like lions out of wolves and roaring. Ahmed Shah's son Tamar and his eldest general Jahan Khan were deported to Lahore Although after the battle of Panipat, Durrani launched a vicious attack on the Singhs and invaded the country in February, he could do no harm to the Singhs. They were very strong now. They rose with more courage and fury than ever before and in the year 6 The great separation of the Durranis in the Malwa region was blown away and the whole area became forever free from the Mughals and Durranis. The following year, Misldar Sardar marched on Lahore and captured the Punjab capital on the auspicious day of April after Baisakhi, and the valiant soldiers of Punjab liberated their country from hundreds of years of slavery. Thus, according to the Nihang's bat, from the holy land of Punjab:

Ahmad Shah Durrani twice again tried to establish government in the Punjab but the Singhs did not allow him to set foot there and he passed away in despair.

At the end of the eighteenth century, when Shah Zaman Durrani of Afghanistan attempted to occupy the Punjab, Ranjit Singh of the Sukkarchakkia misl, with a few comrades from Gujranwala, challenged him to sit down in the fort of Lahore. Durrani lost his footing against the Singhs.

Instead of looking at Punjab, he decided to return to Afghanistan. Seeing the courage of Sardar Ranjit Singh, the Hindu, Muslim and Sikh chiefs of Lahore came to him in unison. At his request, Ranjit Singh came and occupied Lahore, and put all his fears into making the Punjab a strong state, and in a short time extended its borders from Sindh to Tibet and from Khyber to Jamuna.

When Maharaja ranjit singh began to unite the Punjab in the early nineteenth century, the area of Lahore was surrounded on all sides by hostile territories. Holi Ranjit Singh modified Chada Pahar and annexed Multan and Bahawalpur, conquered Kashmir and conquered other areas.

The region north-west across the Indus was originally a stronghold of danger to the Punjab. India but all attacks were from this side. Therefore, deeming it necessary to occupy the area to maintain peace in the Punjab, Maharaja Ranjit Singh marched towards Peshawar across the Indus and annexed the area to the Punjab. At that time there was a mare of Afghanistan. By conquering it, Maharaja Ranjit Singh made it a part of the Punjab.

Thus the Punjab from Khyber to Jamna and from Sindh to Tibet was to be an invaluable asset of the Singhs to India. How the valiant soldiers of Punjab sacrificed their lives, fought against the enemies, gladly made sacrifices and maintained the hanging mark of their pride to conquer this area and keep it a part of Punjab. Hari Singh Nalva is the next meeting of the readers.

Sardar Hari Singh, the protagonist of these characters, was born in the house of Sardar Gurdial Singh on the plains of Shukarchakkia Misl in Gujranwala Sammat 2 B.C., AD. He was eleven years younger than Sardar Ranjit Singh of that misl. Hari Singh was only seven years old when his father passed away and he was brought up in the house of his uncles.

It was a time of wars and battles. Sardar Ranjit Singh's drum everywhere. It was ringing. He had captured Lahore.

He had become the Maharaja. Jammu was new, Sialkot, Gujarat, Pindi Bhattiyan, Daska he had conquered, Multan had accepted. The territory of Amritsar cannabis and highlands had been annexed by the Maharaja and friendship had been established with the British. At this time, Hari Singh, a fifteen-year-old Shakeel youth with a full-bodied, full-bodied and handsome figure, for the first time came to the royal court in the spring of Sammat 5 and joined the ranks of the jawans. The oldest names in the world were defeated. Seeing this, Maharaja Ranjit singh was so pleased that he placed it among his special scholars. Just a few months later, Hari Singh grabbed a leopard by the jaws and attacked it one day. Then Hari Singh quickly cut off his head with a sword. Seeing this, the Maharaja appointed him the next day as the chief officer of a platoon of eight hundred cavalry and infantry called Ber-Dil.

Sardar Hari Singh showed great bravery in the battle of Kar in 1942 and the noisy young Rajman's men captured Nawab Qutbuddin Khan alive and presented him to the Maharaja. Sardar Hari Singh, who went to blow up the fort of Multan in the year 2000, was seriously injured, but soon joined the campaign of sweet-tiwana and earned the reputation of refining the feet of the high! With the capture of the fort of Attack in July 5 AD, and especially with Sardar Dost Mohammad Khan, the heroism shown in the battle, Hari Singh fell in love with them.

 Sardar Hari Singh and Baba Phula Singh were prominent figures in the Akali's campaign and final victory. With this almost the whole of Punjab came together in the line of Ranjit Singh's reign. Now it was only a matter of time before the conquest of the area which in ancient times was a part of India but with the passage of time the Pathans occupied and separated it.

This was the hilly region of Kashmir and the area across the Indus in Peshawar. Maharaja Ranjit Singh first turned his attention to Kashmir. The atrocities of the Pathan rulers had been raging for a long time.

After the Baisakhi of the year, Kashmir was invaded and within three months, the Maharaja conquered Srinagar. After some other arrangements, Hari Singh was appointed governor of the place. Satisfied with their national administration, the Maharaja granted the sardar the right to use his name. This was a unique blessing which the Maharaja had not bestowed on any other chief or his princes.
After the conquest of Mangli, Mugher and Dera caste, Sardar Hari Singh Hazare was appointed governor. Here he built a fort Harikrishnan Garh And inhabited the city of Haripur which still stands in his memory.

By this time Sardar Yar Mohammad Khan of Pathan had accepted Maharaja Ranjit Singh's offer and he would take up the matter with the Punjab government. When his elder brother Mohammad Azim Khan captured Peshawar in February, Sardar Hari Singh stopped his army at Attack and soon Maharaja Ranjit Singh himself arrived. Mohammad Azam Khan fled in defeat and the whole frontier region accepted the government's offer.

In the year 6, Sardar Hari Singh went on a campaign of Katochis and defeated Syed Ahmed Barelvi by a landslide. From this

Later, Hazare himself came again and got Panja Sahib to serve Hasan-Abdal.

Although Yar Mohammad Khan was appointed by the Maharaja in Peshawar, there was no complete peace in the area. The brothers and friends of Yar Hamid Khan himself were on the lookout for an opportunity not to allow the Pathani area west of Sindh and Peshawar to remain among the Sikhs. This obviously meant that they could make secret p reparations against Punjab whenever they wanted without anyone knowing and would seize the opportunity and attack whenever the stakes were high. The same thing has been happening since ancient times in the north-west. It was a political mistake to allow this perpetual threat to remain on the head of the Punjab which Maharaja Ranjit Singh did not want to allow to remain. He therefore sent orders to Sardar Hari Singh Nalva to establish his direct rule over Peshawar. In Chamkanni, the Pathans had set up fronts, but it was not easy to resist Sardar Hari Singh. The Pathans were defeated and on 5 May Sardar Hari Singh took complete control of Peshawar and extended the border of Punjab to Khyber. Pleased with its administration, the Maharaja allowed them to issue their own coin here as well.

An attempt to liberate Peshawar from the Singhs was made by Mohammad Akbar Khan, son of Amir Dost Mohammad Khan, king of Kabul, in the year 7. The battle took place in the field of Jamrud in which Sardar Hari Singh was martyred on 2nd April, but is rohab and dominance was so strong on the

Pathans and the Singhs drew their swords in such a way that the field remained in the hands of Khalsa and Peshawar The area remained a part of Punjab. Not only that Although six years have passed since the martyrdom of Sardar Hari Singh and many more heroes have passed away during this period, he has not yet been able to muster the unparalleled bravery and ability to subdue and control the north-west of the Punjab. It is still a common occurrence in Pathani area and Pathan mothers use the name Hari Singh to intimidate their bullying and naughty children. By saying
Silent children, green rage-silent letter, green [Hari Singh] is coming

A description of the battles of the Bir warriors and their heroism And there is a special form of poetry in Punjabi to sing the praises of fearlessness.

The glory of these scripts lies in the fact with achievements of Hari Singh Nalva with a pro-Punjab sentiment.
The most dramatic and compassionate image of this war poem, describes the victory of Hari Singh Nalva in the battle of Jamrud by beheading him. The whole imagination of the poet
Has been very successful in depicting the historical clock in which Punjab .The armies have permanently stopped the attacks from the northwest. In these letters for patriotism and protection of one's honor There is an inexhaustible motivation to make a great sacrifice. The hour of crisis today Its text gives us the strength to fight for the protection of India.